NATIONAL GEOGRAPHIC
READING EXPEDITIONS®

IMMIGRATION

Isabel's Story
From Guatemala to Georgia

By Julia Schaffer

Illustrated by Graham Kennedy

PICTURE CREDITS

Page borders © Digital Vision/Getty Images;
4 Mapping Specialists, Ltd.; 5 (top) © Dave G. Houser/
Corbis; 5 (bottom) © Charles & Josette Lenars/
Corbis; 60 © Richard I'Anson/Lonely Planet
Images; 61 (top) © Frans Lemmens/Getty Images;
61 (bottom) © Suzy Bennett/Alamy; 62 (top) © Dave G.
Houser/Corbis; 62 (bottom) © Carlos Lopez-Barillas/
Corbis; 64 © Private Collection/Bridgeman Art
Library (top); © Richard Cummins/Corbis (bottom).

PUBLISHED BY THE NATIONAL
GEOGRAPHIC SOCIETY

Produced through the worldwide resources of the
National Geographic Society, John M. Fahey, Jr.,
President and Chief Executive Officer;
Gilbert M. Grosvenor, Chairman of the Board.

PREPARED BY NATIONAL GEOGRAPHIC
SCHOOL PUBLISHING

Sheron Long, Chief Executive Officer; Samuel
Gesumaria, President; Francis Downey, Vice
President and Publisher; Richard Easby, Editorial
Manager; Anne M. Stone, Editor; Margaret
Sidlosky, Director of Design and Illustrations;
Jim Hiscott, Design Manager; Cynthia Olson,
Ruth Ann Thompson, Art Directors; Matt
Wascavage, Director of Publishing Services;
Lisa Pergolizzi, Production Manager.

MANUFACTURING AND QUALITY CONTROL

Christopher A. Liedel, Chief Financial Officer;
Phillip L. Schlosser, Vice President; Clifton M.
Brown III, Director.

CONSULTANT

Mary Anne Wengel

BOOK DESIGN

Artful Doodlers and Insight Design Concepts Ltd.

Published by the National Geographic Society
1145 17th Street N.W.
Washington, D.C. 20036-4688

Product #4U1005081
ISBN: 978-1-4263-5074-0

Printed in Mexico

11 10 09 08 07
10 9 8 7 6 5 4 3 2 1

CONTENTS

LEAVING HOME

The United States is a nation of immigrants. These are people who have moved to a new place, leaving the country where they were born. Some people have come to escape from wars, conflict, or hunger at home. Others have come to find freedom and new opportunities. Whatever the reason, this country has grown thanks to waves of immigrants. One of these waves started in Guatemala in the 1980s.

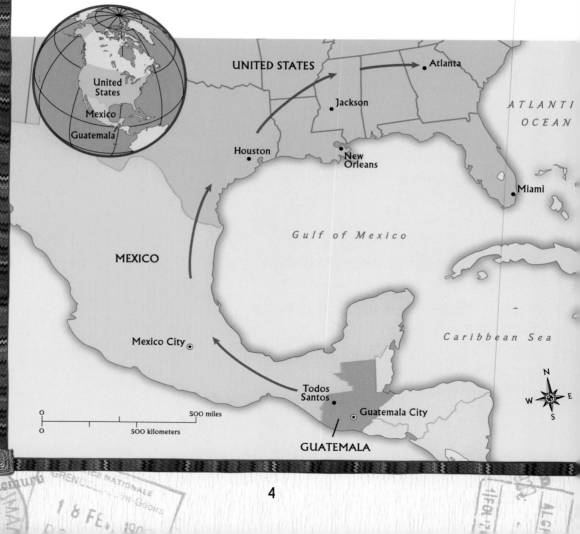

GUATEMALA

Geography Guatemala is a country in Central America. It has a rich and varied terrain. This includes mountains, volcanoes, forests, and coastland. A chain of mountains splits Guatemala into northern and southern regions. The land is very fertile.

The People Most Guatemalans live in the highlands or near the southern coast. Many work on farms or plantations. They grow crops such as cotton, corn, coffee, bananas, and sugarcane. The official language of Guatemala is Spanish, but 20 different Maya languages are also spoken.

THE PERALTA FAMILY

Hector Peralta

Hector is Isabel's father. In Guatemala, he picked cotton and coffee beans for a wealthy landowner. In Georgia, he has found work on a farm two hours from Atlanta.

Gloria Peralta

Gloria is Isabel's older sister. Gloria has stayed behind in Guatemala. Her husband is missing and she is searching for him.

Isabel Peralta

Isabel is a sixth grader in Atlanta, Georgia. She and her parents have just moved from Guatemala. Isabel wants to fit in and make friends, but doesn't talk much in class. She misses the familiar sights, sounds, and smells of her home in Guatemala.

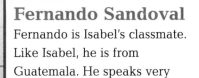

Fernando Sandoval

Fernando is Isabel's classmate. Like Isabel, he is from Guatemala. He speaks very little English, so Isabel has to translate for him.

Maria Peralta

Maria is Isabel's mother. In Guatemala, she was a weaver and she tended the family's garden. In Atlanta, she cleans houses and apartments. She has not yet learned to speak English.

CHAPTER 1

Multiplying Fractions

The teacher began writing fractions on the blackboard. That was a relief. In math, Isabel could think in numbers. No English was necessary. Thinking in English all the time was exhausting. Isabel welcomed the break.

Back in Guatemala, Isabel had been great at English. When she arrived in the United States she'd been excited to be surrounded by the language everywhere she looked. Billboards, television screens, street signs. English was everywhere. Isabel was proud to be able to speak the language. She could help her mother, who knew only a few words of English.

But now, in her sixth grade classroom in Atlanta, Georgia, speaking English wasn't a special trick. It wasn't even something that got her good grades and a reputation for being smart. It was just what was expected. And the English-speaking part of her was tired. Tired of learning new words. Tired of people asking her to repeat herself because they didn't understand her accent. Isabel sometimes longed to hear everyone speaking Spanish like they did in Guatemala. Numbers, at least, were a language that everyone shared.

Isabel's mother, Maria, wondered what had gotten into her. Isabel wasn't the same as she'd been in Guatemala. She was quieter, more reserved. But no one at school knew. They didn't know anything about her. Except that she was good at math.

If she weren't so tired of all the new things in her life, Isabel might find that funny. In Guatemala, she hadn't thought she was that good at math. She had relied on her older sister, Gloria, to help her with math homework all the time.

"What is 1/2 times 1/2? Anyone? Teddy?" said the teacher, Mr. Mann.

"Uh, 1?"

"No. Remember, we're not adding 1/2 and 1/2. We're multiplying. If we were adding, you're right, the answer would be 1. Anyone else?"

"1/4," Isabel wrote on her paper.

"Yes, Marcus?" said Mr. Mann.

"1/4?"

"That's right." Mr. Mann reminded Isabel of a tall and delicate bird. He seemed to speak his own language too, chuckling at things no one else found funny. And what about his name? Mr. Mann. In Guatemala last names told you about a person. She knew just by looking at him that he was a man. Isabel's Spanish name was Peralta, a reference to the highlands where she lived. Her Maya name, Yaq'ol, meant that the women in her family had been midwives. They helped women deliver babies.

"How about 1/4 times 1/4?" asked the teacher.

Isabel scribbled on her paper, "1/16." Then she had a strange thought. Like all her thoughts and dreams, it came to her in Mam, the Maya language she spoke with her parents. *Here in Atlanta, I'm half of myself. I left the other half in Guatemala. The longer I stay here, the Guatemalan half will multiply by itself and I'll become one quarter. Then the quarter will multiply and I'll become a sixteenth of myself. If I keep multiplying, the Guatemalan part will become less and less.*

"And 1/3 times 1/4?" Isabel wrote "1/12" on her paper. "Anyone? Isabel?"

"1/12," she answered.

"Can you speak up?" said Mr. Mann.

Isabel took a deep breath and almost shouted, "1/12!"

Ryan, the boy sitting next to her, pretended to be shocked. *"Wow,"* he whispered, *"she talks!"*

"Thank you, Isabel."

Isabel didn't know if Mr. Mann was ignoring Ryan or if he hadn't heard the comment. One student heard it. Tracy Hill was bossy at times, but Isabel could tell she had a good heart. With her bright red hair, Tracy was often the first person Isabel saw when she walked into the room. "Of course she talks," Tracy hissed. "And not just in English. She speaks two languages. How many do you speak, Ryan?" Tracy turned around in her seat and smiled at Isabel. *Actually I speak three.* Isabel thought. *English, Spanish, and Mam.* She smiled back at Tracy. Or she meant to. In her heart she smiled, but it was hard to make herself actually do it. She looked down at her paper. *You're not going to make friends this way,* she told herself.

On her way out of school, Isabel saw a girl who looked just like her. Maybe she was from Guatemala. She looked around Isabel's age, maybe a little younger. She wore her black hair in pigtails. Her eyes were brown. Something about them looked familiar. She looked like the girls from home who lived in the city, the ones whose parents paid Isabel's father to pick coffee and cotton.

Isabel watched the girl's pigtails swing. Where was she from? Had she come on a bus through Mexico and over the border into Texas? Had she flown in an airplane? Did

she speak Spanish at home? Had she left, like Isabel, because the **civil war** was making Guatemala unsafe? Isabel's excitement rose. There were so many questions she would like to ask the girl.

"Wait for me!" the girl screamed as the school bus closed its doors. Just like that, she seemed to change before Isabel's eyes. She wasn't Guatemalan. Isabel could hear it in her voice and see it in the way she ran toward the bus. She was American.

Disappointed, Isabel turned left out of the schoolyard. She started thinking about Guatemala and why her family had left to come to the United States.

- -

civil war – a war between people living in the same country

Just a few months ago, a new president had come to power in Guatemala. He was a **dictator**, and he had begun to force the people to accept a new kind of government. Many Guatemalans had started to fight back. In the town of Todos Santos where Isabel lived, they had heard rumors that villages in the mountains had been burned to the ground. The president's soldiers were destroying the villages. They believed that people in the villages opposed the new president. Isabel's father had decided that it was no longer safe to stay in Guatemala. He had moved to the United States. He then had quickly saved enough money to move Isabel and her mother too.

Isabel was deep in thought as she approached a crosswalk. Suddenly, a truck pulled up alongside her.

"Excuse me," called a voice.

Isabel turned toward the voice. She saw a man in uniform and froze. He reminded her of the soldiers back home in Guatemala.

"Have you seen a dog around here? Chocolate brown? Like a Labrador? It ran away this morning."

Isabel just stared at the man. She couldn't speak. All she could think about was the uniform and the soldiers with their guns.

"Do you speak English?" the man asked.

----

dictator – a person who rules by force or fear

Isabel shook her head and took a step backward.

"Well thanks anyway," said the man and drove away.

Isabel stood still, her heart pounding, her legs weak. The man in uniform had caught her by surprise. She shuddered and shook herself as if to get rid of the bad memory. Suddenly a dog barked close by. Isabel saw a small opening between two buildings. She stepped in and found herself on a narrow alley, hidden from the street. There she saw what the police had been looking for.

She approached the dog and knelt down beside it, rubbing its head and ears. *"Hola, perro,"* she said in Spanish. "Hi, puppy." She rested her head on the dog's brown fur. You're safe now," she said. "The police have gone away."

CHAPTER 2

Current Events

"Isabel," said Mr. Mann leaning over her desk. "This is Fernando Sandoval." Isabel looked at the boy. She caught his wide eyes wandering around the classroom, with its books, posters, and signs in English on every wall. "He's from Guatemala."

"Really?" she asked quickly.

"Yes," Mr. Mann laughed. "Really. You won't be the only one anymore."

Isabel caught the boy's eye and smiled. *"Hola,"* she said.

"Hola," he answered.

Mr. Mann continued, "Fernando should be in seventh grade, but he doesn't speak English. We've placed him in this class so that you can translate for him. You won't mind helping him, will you?"

"That's fine," Isabel said. She knew from going to the post office, the grocery store, and everywhere else with her mom that translating for someone is hard work. But she didn't care. Here at last was someone who would know who she was.

"*¿Qué es lo que dijo?*" Fernando asked Isabel what the teacher had said after Mr. Mann had turned his back.

"He said that you're older, but you're in this class so I can translate for you."

"Yeah, I studied at a German school."

"Oh, I thought you're from Guatemala."

"I am. From Guatemala City, but my parents sent me to a school where we studied German instead of English."

"Oh. You should have moved to Germany."

He laughed. "That's exactly what I told my parents. But then we would have needed an airplane."

"I hear it's pretty crowded in Guatemala City."

"You've never been there?"

"I went with my dad when I was young, but I don't remember it. I'm from a small town called Todos Santos."

"Oh, you're a country girl," said Fernando.

"Yes. I miss the lime trees."

There was a rustle among the students. "Why's everyone standing up?"

"This is where we say the Pledge of Allegiance."

"The what?"

"It's where we promise to be true to the United States."

"Wow, I sure am an American now, " Fernando said.

"Yeah, a Spanish-speaking American."

"A cheese-pizza-eating and baseball-loving American," he said. Isabel laughed.

At lunchtime, Isabel showed Fernando where the cafeteria was. When they got to the cafeteria, they took a seat next to the window and opened their lunch boxes. Isabel had corn tortillas and black beans. Fernando had a turkey sandwich. He looked at the bread suspiciously. "My mom wants me to eat American food. That way I'll get used to everything faster."

"Not my mom," said Isabel. "She's afraid the sky will fall if I don't have tortillas for breakfast, lunch, and dinner. When I see what everyone else is eating, I get curious and want to try American food. Want to switch?"

They traded lunches.

"I love homemade tortillas," said Fernando with his mouth full. "So, Isabel, how did a country girl like you end up in a big city like Atlanta?"

"We probably came for the same reasons," laughed Isabel. "But if you want my life story I will tell you," she said, more seriously.

Isabel felt she could talk openly to Fernando. He was from her country and she felt comfortable telling her story in Spanish.

"You know about the Guatemalan army burning villages in the mountains as they searched for enemies of the president?" asked Isabel.

Fernando nodded.

"One hot afternoon I was with my mother and sister, Gloria, in Todos Santos. I remember hearing a truck in the distance. And then another. And then another. So many that I couldn't hear them separately, just a whoosh, like an approaching storm. My father ran up and told us all to get in our house and shut the door. We knew that the president's army had finally come to our town. We waited, not knowing what would happen. We heard the army trucks pull into our village. We heard the truck doors slam and the voices of soldiers.

"Suddenly a fist pounded on our door. My father opened the door. Outside were two soldiers in uniform and with guns at their sides. One of them asked my father if there was anyone else in the house. My father said no. But the two soldiers came in and searched anyway. They even searched the loft where we stored our corn.

"The soldiers then told us all to walk to the church in the center of Todos Santos. All the people were pushed inside the church. The soldiers brought people from all around, from the town and the surrounding countryside. They packed us in and closed the door. Everyone was there. In a way, it was like our town fiesta, but of course it was really the opposite. People were crying and praying. We were in a church so it was the right place to pray for our lives."

"Wow!" said Fernando. "You must have been scared."

"We thought we would be killed," said Isabel. "My mother held on to my sister and me the whole night but we didn't speak. We were afraid to do anything that would make the soldiers notice us. I knew my sister was scared. We hadn't seen her husband, Romeo, for more than a day. He had been working in the fields outside the village when the soldiers came.

"By the time morning arrived, we were so afraid that we could barely breathe. It was as if the air in the church had turned to poison. We waited for the soldiers to come for us, but they didn't.

"Finally, my school principal opened the door a crack and looked out. The army was gone. They were nowhere to be seen. We all cried and hugged each other. We were so thankful to be alive. But other people were in a terrible panic. Many men were missing; they hadn't been brought to the church. People ran from the church to look for their missing loved ones. My sister was one of them.

"My father said it was a warning to Todos Santos, and he didn't want to wait for another one. He left almost immediately for the United States."

"Without you?" Fernando asked.

"He got a visa to work here on a farm. He came ahead of us and then sent money and instructions. We arrived two months ago, but we still haven't seen him. My mom says he is just a couple of hours from here, but there is a lot of work right now and he can't get away. Anyway, he is coming to Atlanta for a visit in a week. Then our family will be almost whole again."

"What happened to your sister?"

"She stayed behind."

"And her husband?"

"No one knows. The police said he disappeared. My mother believes we won't find him, but my sister is still hoping. My mother and sister had a terrible fight when she refused to come here. My mother made me say goodbye as though I'll never see her again." Isabel stopped speaking. Her face clouded over.

"That's not true," said Fernando trying to comfort her. "You'll see her again. You will."

"We should go back to class," Isabel said. "The bell is going to ring." As they gathered up their things and headed for the door, she apologized. "I'm sorry. I didn't ask about why you left."

"I'll give you the short version," Fernando said. "My father was a **journalist** in Guatemala City. When the new president came to power, my father was very upset. He wrote articles that challenged the government. Sometimes he was critical of the president. After all, his job was to make sure people knew the truth. He began to receive threats. Then a friend in the government warned my father that there was a plot to kill him. We left in the night and took almost nothing."

----

journalist – someone who writes for a newspaper or magazine

Isabel and Fernando returned to the classroom and took their seats. Tracy, who sat in front of Isabel, turned around and smiled at Fernando. "I'm Tracy Hill," she said. "Class president and future lawyer. What brings you to our school?" Fernando looked puzzled and turned to Isabel, who laughed.

"He doesn't speak English," Isabel explained. "Only Spanish and German."

"I wish I spoke Spanish," Tracy sighed.

"What are you guys talking about?" Fernando asked.

"You," Isabel teased. "She said she thinks you're cute." Fernando narrowed his eyes playfully.

"Where is Fernando from?" Tracy asked.

"He's from Guatemala like me," said Isabel. "His family escaped."

"What? Why?" Tracy asked.

Oh no! I said too much, Isabel thought desperately.

"Is that really true?" Tracy searched Fernando's face as though he might understand her if only she raised her eyebrows high enough.

"What is she saying?" Fernando asked.

"I told her you escaped, and she was very surprised."

"I can see that."

"She asked if it was really true."

"Of course it's true. *¡Sí! Yeees!*" He said the English word in an exaggerated way.

"So, you *do* speak English," said Tracy.

Fernando looked to Isabel, "Huh?"

Just then Mr. Mann cleared his throat. "Current events," he announced. "I'm going to ask you to work in pairs on a project that will be due next week. With your partner, you'll choose a current events topic. You will research your topic and prepare a presentation to make before the class. And, because life is not a popularity contest, I've chosen partners for you."

Isabel translated quietly for Fernando. Mr. Mann had paired the two of them. That was good. Fernando was fun to talk to. He made her feel relaxed and even just a little bit happy. She could tell him about the current events the class had discussed earlier that week: elections, sports, and new buildings going up in downtown Atlanta.

"So we're working together?" Fernando asked when Mr. Mann was finished.

"Yes."

"Perfect," he said.

"Yes," Isabel agreed. "What topic shall we choose?"

"I know exactly what we should talk about. Can't you guess?" he asked.

"No, what?" She was surprised he already knew enough about current events to choose a topic.

"The war."

"In Guatemala?"

"*Sí.*"

"We can't talk about that," Isabel whispered.

"*¿Por qué no?*" he asked her. Why not?

"It's in another country."

"Did he say we have to talk about this country?"

"No . . ." Isabel hesitated.

"So what then?"

"So we shouldn't talk about that. People don't want to hear about it."

"What do you mean? That girl wanted to know," he said, pointing to Tracy.

"We'll get in trouble."

"Why would we get in trouble? With who?"

"They won't believe us, Fernando. Trust me."

"What's with you?"

"Nothing. I just . . . we can't choose that topic."

"We can't *not* choose it. What are you so worried about?" Fernando said firmly.

Isabel opened her mouth, but she didn't have a good answer, just a very strong feeling. Then, lowering her voice she said, "Don't you know it's dangerous to talk about that? Don't you, of all people, know? You who had to leave home because of it? Your father would have been put in prison or even killed if he had stayed in Guatemala. It is best to keep our mouths shut."

"But we are not in Guatemala. Don't you know that America has laws protecting people who speak out? Here it's safe to talk about things."

"My father doesn't tell people on the farm he's from Guatemala," Isabel said. "He tells them he's from Mexico."

Fernando threw up his hands. "What does that have to do with anything?"

"People here don't want to know about our problems. They want us to fit in. It's when people attract attention to themselves that bad things happen. You know, the nail that sticks up gets hit on the head."

"Why are you whispering?" asked Fernando. "No one here speaks Spanish."

"Okay, everyone," Mr. Mann called out. "Wrap it up. You can continue speaking with your partners at the end of class. Now let's get back to our social studies book. Please open it to page 46." Isabel held her book so Fernando could see it too. She tried to translate what Mr. Mann said, but her mind was racing. She had to convince him to pick a different topic. She bit her lip. She didn't know how she was going to do it.

CHAPTER 3

Learning to Be Brave

With her eyes closed Isabel listened to a familiar sound, the slapping of her mother's hands as she made tortillas. Isabel knew she should get up and help her mother. *One more minute,* she told herself. *One more minute of pretending I'm in Guatemala. Then I will get up and start my day in Atlanta.* She turned on her side and felt the weave of her sleeping mat against her arm. It was the mat she'd always slept on in Guatemala. Now, in Atlanta, she lived on the third floor of an apartment building. She could hear television shows in the apartment below instead of the sounds of nature. Americans, she knew, didn't sleep on mats. A few blocks from her apartment, there was a store that sold beds as tall as tables. Her mother had offered to buy a bed, but Isabel liked her mat.

"Isa," her mother called. Isabel's stomach tightened. One minute was up. If ever there was a day she wished she could float away it was today, the day she and Fernando were supposed to give their report. "I'm up, Mama. Here I come."

For the last week Isabel and Fernando had worked together preparing the report. He had finally talked Isabel into doing their report on the civil war in Guatemala. The United States wasn't like Guatemala. There was freedom of speech here. People could have different opinions and say them out loud. Fernando had argued that they should give their new home a chance. Isabel had reluctantly agreed. But secretly she was scared that their teacher would be angry and they would get into trouble.

Isabel walked to the kitchen of their one-room apartment. There was a calendar pinned to the wall. On the twelfth of the month Isabel's mother had drawn a red heart and written HECTOR, the name of Isabel's father, inside it. Isabel's father was coming home in a few days. Isabel kissed her mother and packed some tortillas into two brown paper bags, one for Isabel to take to school and one for her mother to take to work.

Before coming to the United States, Isabel's mother had tended the family's farm and made cloth to sell. Now she cleaned houses and apartments filled with things neither she nor Isabel had ever seen before. She came home each afternoon describing machines for heating and cleaning, mixing and chopping. Microwaves, dishwashers, and washing machines. There were none of these machines in Todos Santos. Before coming to the United States, Isabel had never taken food from a refrigerator or flushed a toilet. Now she did both every day.

Their first week in Atlanta had been like a strange dream. She and her mother had jumped at every sound. Honking car horns. Squealing brakes. They waited until there were no cars in sight before they crossed the street. Using hand gestures and simple English, one of their neighbors had shown them how to use the sink and the shower. She had explained the freezer and even the front door key. Isabel had never used one before.

"Any word from Dad?" Isabel asked.

"Not yet. He's scheduled to arrive Friday afternoon."

Isabel's stomach tightened. "I wish it were already Friday," she said.

"También," her mother agreed. She didn't know that Isabel had an extra reason for wishing the days would pass quickly.

When Mr. Mann called Fernando and Isabel to the front of the classroom, Isabel's heart was pounding. She could see that Fernando was nervous too. He had an intense, almost burning look in his eye. Teddy and Ryan had just finished a report on the 1982 tropical storm season, describing all the damage caused by Hurricane Debby. Before that, Monique and Michelle had spoken about the new craze for diet soda, and Tracy and Jordan had given a presentation on the Martin Luther King, Jr., National Historic Site not far from their school.

Now it was Isabel and Fernando's turn. With her back to the chalkboard, Isabel looked out at her classmates. She knew their names, but not much else about them. And what did they know about her?

"Ready?" Fernando asked. Isabel forced a smile. She reminded herself to speak loudly. People here were always asking her to repeat herself.

Fernando opened the presentation by saying. *"Me llamó es Fernando. Haslaremos de Guatemala."*

Isabel told the class, "I will now translate what Fernando said." She took a deep breath and repeated what Fernando had said. "My name is Fernando. We will now talk to you about Guatemala."

Fernando continued in Spanish, "You may not know that there is a war in my country. It has been going on for more than twenty years. In order to understand what is happening today, you need to know some history. In 1944, a new president was elected. He supported a political group called the **communists**. The communists wanted to change many things. Some people did not like

---

communists – people who believe that all wealth should be divided among all people equally

this. In 1954, they overthrew the government by force. The new government was not good. They took away people's freedoms. Some members of the armed forces decided to rebel against the new government. They formed their own armies to fight the government. They are called **guerrillas.** This is the origin of the war that drove Isabel and me from our homes."

Isabel repeated in English what Fernando had said. He watched her speak and smiled encouragingly.

Fernando went on in Spanish. "In March of this year, a new president came to power. The president got rid of parts of the government. He said they were not needed. He began to use violence against anyone who did not

---

guerrillas – people who choose to fight against a government or other ruling power

agree with him. He has been very violent toward the native people. The native people of Guatemala are called the Maya. They are a Native American people just like the Native American people of North America. Isabel and her family are Maya."

Fernando stopped talking. While Isabel was translating, he held up a large collage. It was covered with newspaper articles and pictures of Guatemalan cities: Antigua, Guatemala City, and Huehuetenango. Fernando propped the poster on the chalkboard. From behind Mr. Mann's desk, he pulled out another poster with more news articles and images of villages before and after army raids. One of them was of Isabel's own town, Todos Santos.

Without thinking she blurted out, "That's my home! That's where I live!" and pointed to the picture. The class all stared at her.

Fernando looked at her with a twinkle in his eye. "I added a little surprise," he said in Spanish.

"I see," said Isabel. She turned back to the class.

"Excuse me," she said, her face burning. "Fernando and I would now like to tell you about our own experiences and why we came to the United States." She stood beside the photo of the church in Todos Santos. The photo reminded her of the day the soldiers came to her village. She began to tell the class her story, "This is the church where the army took us the day they raided our town. They came to scare us, to try to warn us against joining the guerrillas. But we didn't want to be part of any fighting. We just wanted to live in peace.

"A few weeks later, the army returned. This time, they stayed. They took over part of our school and made an office there. They gave every man over 16 an army uniform and made them walk the streets at night. These new soldiers were forced to punish people who were out after dark. Our town became a different place. Everyone was afraid—afraid to say anything, afraid of the night."

Isabel looked at her classmates. No one was fidgeting. No one was looking down or passing notes. They were listening. She whispered to Fernando, "Tell them about your father."

Fernando cleared his throat. "My father is a journalist," he said in Spanish. "His job is to tell people what's really happening. Our country is not a free place to live right now. And yet almost nobody outside Guatemala knows this." Isabel translated word for word.

Fernando continued. "My father tried to tell the truth in these newspaper articles. He wrote all of these," he said, gesturing toward the posters. "Because of that, his life was threatened. That's why we came here."

Mr. Mann stood up. Was he going to make them stop? Was he going to say it wasn't true? Isabel waited anxiously for the teacher to speak. "This is a very powerful presentation," he said. "I wonder if anyone would like to ask any questions."

Three hands shot up. "Isabel," Monique asked, "did your father or your brothers have to join the army?"

"Fortunately my father was already in the United States by the time the army returned. I have no brothers."

"Did you have to leave in secret?" asked Michelle.

"Yes," said Isabel. "Before my father left he got visas and instructed my mother and me to wait until he sent money. He also told us not to tell anyone we were leaving." Isabel thought of her friends Rogelia and Desiderio. She hadn't seen them since her family left Todos Santos. They'd been friends for as long as she could remember. Ever since they were old enough, they used to collect firewood for the widows in town. She had left without saying goodbye to them.

"The class wants to know if you left in secret," she told Fernando.

"Sí, nos fuimos a media noche."

"He said his family left in the night." Her mind wandered again. She hoped Gloria had explained everything to her friends.

"Do you miss your country?" Teddy asked. Fernando nodded forcefully when Isabel translated.

"Me too," said Isabel. "I love Guatemala. I love the people and the places. If these pictures were in color,

you'd see that everything is green. We grow our own food—corn, beans, and squash—and it tastes so fresh."

"Then why did you leave?" asked Jordan.

"We weren't safe there. Here we hope we can be safe. But the truth is," Isabel said, even though she didn't know if anyone would understand, "it's hard to feel safe when you're used to so much danger."

"Let's take one last question," said Mr. Mann. "Tracy? Your hand is up."

"How can we help?" she said.

Isabel translated the question for Fernando who looked thoughtful, but said nothing. Isabel didn't know what to say either.

"That's a great question," Mr. Mann interjected. "But it seems we'll have to keep thinking about that one. Let's give a round of applause to all of today's presenters." Mr. Mann asked Isabel and Fernando to stay behind after class. Though she wasn't sure what Mr. Mann would say, Isabel knew now that Fernando had been right. She was glad they'd made a presentation on the war in Guatemala.

"Thank you both for that presentation," Mr. Mann said, as the rest of the class filed out. "It was very brave of you to speak about your experiences. I understand that in Guatemala you couldn't speak freely, but here you can. And I hope you will continue to. We learn a lot from what you have to say."

"He said we were very brave," Isabel explained to Fernando on their way to music.

"You were very brave," Fernando said and he punched her playfully on the shoulder.

CHAPTER 4

Bad News

Isabel ran down two flights of stairs. She felt like she could run the whole way home, and not just because her dad would be there waiting for her. Ever since she and Fernando had given their report, school had become a different place. People wanted to know things about her life in Guatemala. It was almost as though they hadn't noticed her until she stood up in front of the class.

Isabel turned left out of the schoolyard and there was her father. "Papa!" she shouted. She ran to him and hugged him tight. His back was so wide her arms barely fit around.

"How did you find me here?" she asked, still hugging.

"Lucky guess."

"But how did you get to my school?"

"By way of Mexico," he answered, grinning.

"Papaaaaa," she teased. "I need to send you to joke school, your jokes are so bad. You look—" she took a long look at him. "You still look like my dad." He kissed the top of her head.

"Are you hungry?" she asked. "I didn't finish my lunch. You can have some if you want."

"Isalita. Your mother stuffed me with tamales."

"Why didn't she come?"

"She's resting."

"Oh?" That didn't sound like her mother. "Is everything okay?"

"Gloria sent a message to me at the farm."

"I wish she'd send me a message, Papa. I miss her." There was a pause. "What?" Isabel asked looking up at her father, stopping them both in their tracks. "Tell me."

"She found Romeo. He's dead."

No! How could her sister's husband be dead? How could he be any way but how she pictured him: whistling a tune and patting their animals on the head. He used to talk to them. When one of the pigs would snort, he'd laugh and say, "I don't believe it. Prove it to me." He did it just to make Isabel laugh.

On the day of Gloria and Romeo's wedding, the house had been decorated with white flowers and Isabel's mother had burned incense. Isabel could see them now, kneeling side by side, receiving their parents' blessing and promising to uphold the traditions of the Maya people until the day they died.

Isabel looked at her father but she quickly turned her head. There were tears in his eyes. She had never seen that before. He took her hand as they walked in silence.

"What happened to him?" Isabel asked.

"I don't know," her father said. They continued walking and holding hands.

Poor Gloria, Isabel thought. She had kept alive a flame of hope. She had believed he would return. What would it be like to stay in that house knowing he would never come home?

"Gloria should come here," she said.

Her father sighed. "Yes. She wants to come now."

"Don't you agree?" questioned Isabel.

"Yes, little one, but not right away. It takes time and money to make this happen."

"But she needs to be with her family."

"I can't leave now when we're harvesting. I can't go with her to Guatemala City for her papers. It took me weeks to arrange for you and your mother to come here." He grew more agitated as he spoke. "A person can't just leave, Isabel. You need permission to enter the United States. And once you get here, you need a job. We need to buy our own food here. We don't wash our clothes in rivers here. Everything takes money. And making money takes time."

"But it's unsafe in Guatemala. That's why you took us out," Isabel said, raising her voice.

"And I will do the same for her, but she needs to wait—you both need to wait—until I can get back there. I can't be in two places at once."

What a strange combination my father is, thought Isabel. *Brave and fearful at the same time.*

They continued to walk in silence. Then her father suddenly stopped. "What's that sound?" he asked. Isabel heard a whimper. She looked around and quickly recognized where they were.

"I know what it is, Papa." She ducked into the space between two buildings and into the hidden alley.
There was the chocolate brown dog, looking mangy.

"*Perro,*" Isabel said. "You've been alone and lost this whole time?"

"Why don't you give her those leftovers?" her father suggested, stroking the dog's ears. Isabel poured a little water into a dent in the ground and placed part of her tortilla beside it. The dog ate gratefully.

"Papa," Isabel said. "We should take the dog to its owner. Poor thing!"

"It's not our problem," he observed.

"A man in uniform was looking for her the other day. I think he was an animal control officer. He reminded me of the soldiers back home. So I didn't tell him where she was. I thought the dog would be better on her own, but I've changed my mind. I think we should take her to the police station. They will be able to contact the animal control office. Maybe they know who her owner is."

"No," said her father. "Someone who speaks English can take care of that."

"I speak English, Papa."

In her mind she saw Fernando watching her. She wasn't in Guatemala anymore and she didn't have to fear the government. "Papa, this dog is lost. No one is caring for it."

Her father spoke sharply, "Why do you want to make trouble, Isabel?"

"I'm not making trouble." She could almost hear the words coming out of Fernando's mouth. "I just want to help. To do the right thing."

"That's not a good enough reason to endanger yourself," said her father.

She knew it: he was afraid. "Papa," she said. Already her voice felt foreign in her throat. She was about to speak to her father in a way she never had before. "We're not in Guatemala. We don't have to be afraid of the police." Her father looked at her silently. "You're the one who taught me to help my neighbors. That's all this is. How can we call America home if we don't do that here?"

"Okay," he said quietly and put his hand on her head.

"Come on, *perro,*" she cooed, luring the animal with bits of food.

Isabel's father tensed up as they approached the police station with the dog. "Quickly, Isabel. Just give them the dog. We don't need to invite them over for tortillas."

"All right, Papa." They opened the door.

"Hello," Isabel said to the first officer she saw. "I think this dog is lost. Can you check to see if it has an owner?" *Otherwise,* she thought to herself, *I'd like to keep it. It would be nice to have a dog again,* though she couldn't imagine how dogs lived in the city with no fields to run in and no farm animals to keep in line.

"Yes," said the officer. "The Animal Control Office gives us a file of missing pets. Look, here is a photo of your dog. Her name is Savannah." The dog looked up at the sound of her name. "Hey, Savannah. Here, pup. We'll give the owner a call."

"Thank you," said Isabel. She hesitated. "Can I ask you a question?"

"Sure can."

"What can someone do if they're trying to leave their country where it's unsafe and come to the United States?"

"I'm no lawyer, but I think if they can prove that their country is unsafe, the United States will give them **asylum.** That means they can move to the United States for protection." Isabel wasn't familiar with that word, but she hoped it was a good thing. "You should talk to a lawyer about your situation."

"Oh." Isabel glanced nervously at her dad even though he didn't speak English. "It isn't my situation," she said. "Just a friend's."

"Okay," the police officer said and reached out to shake her hand. "Thank you for bringing in the dog." Then he extended his hand to her father.

Outside, Isabel sighed happily. "Isn't that why you brought us here, Papa?"

"I don't know what you're talking about," he said. But he was smiling too.

- - - - - - - - - - - -

asylum – protection

CHAPTER 5

A Lesson from Todos Santos

"Tracy," Isabel called. She wanted to catch her friend before homeroom started. "Do you remember when you asked how you could help?" Tracy looked blank. "Remember when Fernando and I gave our report on Guatemala and you asked what you could do?"

"Oh yeah, did you think of something?"

"Yes. It wouldn't be helping a whole town or anything, just a couple of very important people."

"Great," said Tracy.

The bell rang and they began to hurry to class.

"I was thinking we could talk about it at lunch. You want to meet at the table by the windows?" asked Isabel.

"Perfect," said Tracy. "See you there."

As usual, Isabel sat down beside Fernando. "Good morning," she said. He looked up and smiled.

Since it was math, Isabel didn't need to translate much. She could act like a regular student. She passed Fernando a note: "Do you want to have lunch together?" Fernando shrugged. She decided to tell him. "I need to find a safe way to bring my sister here," she wrote. "Her husband has died."

Fernando looked up sharply. "I'm sorry," he whispered. Isabel nodded. Fernando picked up his pencil: "What happened?" he wrote.

"I'll tell you at lunch. We can trade if you want." Fernando gave her a sheepish smile.

Just before the lunch break, Isabel asked to use the bathroom. She ran down to the cafeteria and staked out the table by the big window. In the few minutes before the bell rang, she tried to gather her thoughts.

Fernando and Tracy arrived together and sat down. "Tracy," Isabel said, speaking over her nervousness, "I'm going to start in Spanish and then translate into English."

"Fine by me."

"Okay," Isabel began. "I got this idea because I have a problem that I don't know how to solve. In Todos Santos, we had a special type of government for the town people. It was called a town council. At meetings, people tried to help solve each other's problems. My family and I have nothing like that here, so my idea is to make a town council out of the people I know. Starting with you."

"Brilliant!" Tracy said when she heard the translation.

Isabel couldn't read Fernando's face. He was waiting for more. "For example, Fernando, your father needs a job, he needs to work to support his family, and it would be best if he could find a job as a journalist."

Fernando smiled and nodded gratefully. "What about the other thing?" he asked. "Your thing."

"I'm getting to that. First let me translate."

She did and then continued in English. "The second problem has to do with my sister, Gloria. She needs to leave Guatemala right away. My parents need to talk to a lawyer about getting her out safely. Those are the two main problems I think we need to solve. Do you guys want to add some others? Something that you need or your parents need?"

"Well," said Fernando after Isabel translated, "this is kind of a weird one, but I think my parents need some friends in this country."

"Yes," Isabel agreed. "My parents too. And English lessons as well."

"I could use those," said Fernando.

"I need Spanish lessons," Tracy chimed in once Isabel had translated.

Fernando and Tracy looked at Isabel, waiting for her to go on.

"That's all," she said.

"How did this town council actually solve the problems?" Fernando asked.

"I don't know. I wasn't even old enough yet to go to the meetings."

"Well," Tracy said, without waiting for a translation, "I think these are very important and solvable problems. May I suggest a method?"

"Yes, please," said Isabel, suddenly grateful for her take-charge manner.

"I learned this in student government. First, we write a list of all the things we need. A job for Fernando's father. A lawyer for Gloria. English lessons. Spanish lessons. A community of friends. Next we put them in order of priority. Then we think of all the people and places that could help us. So, for example, a job in journalism. My mother works in a library. Her branch has lots of newspapers and some of them are in different languages. She'll know the Spanish papers. Maybe she'll even know someone who works at one. Also, I heard the principal used to work for a TV station. We should ask him too. We have to talk to everyone we can think of."

Isabel laughed out of sheer nervousness.

"That gives me an idea," said Fernando after hearing the Spanish. "What if Tracy and I trade lessons?"

"Great!" exclaimed Tracy when Isabel told her what Fernando had suggested. There was a pause.

"Tracy," Isabel asked, "Do you know what the word *asylum* means?"

"Asylum!" shouted Fernando, speaking the word with a strong accent. "That's what my parents have!"

Isabel looked surprised. "Since when do you know such a hard English word?

"*Po-lit-i-cal a-sy-lum.* It means that the United States will let you come and stay because your country is unsafe. If you have to leave your country very fast, then you go to the United States border and ask for political asylum. That's what my parents did."

"How do you get it?" asked Isabel, excitedly.

"I don't know exactly. My parents met with a lawyer and then went to a government office. They had to fill out tons of forms," explained Fernando.

"My dad is not going to like that." Isabel sighed and flopped back in her chair.

"Yes, he will. The lawyer they met with spoke Spanish," said Fernando.

"Really?" asked Isabel, spilling her drink in her excitement. "My dad will be able to speak to the lawyer himself and not rely on me."

"I'm sure I can get you her telephone number from my parents," said Fernando.

Gloria could leave, Isabel thought. *She could leave right now.* Her father would think it was too good to be true. What would his objections be? "What about money?" Isabel asked.

Tracy noticed the pause. "Why the silence? Translate."

"I'm thinking if my sister could get asylum, she could leave right away. But I'm sure my father will say she doesn't have enough money."

"So we'll raise the money," said Tracy brightly.

"What do you mean, raise money? How are we going to do that?" asked Isabel.

"Isabel, you're talking to a class president. I know how to raise money."

Isabel smiled, a little perplexed.

"The best ways are to hold a bake sale or throw a party. We might as well do both since airfare is expensive."

"Airfare?"

"If we're going to do this, let's do it right." Tracy grinned. "Is anyone else starving?"

Isabel glanced at the clock. Lunch was almost over and they hadn't touched their food. She reached into her bag and passed Fernando the tortillas. She accepted his turkey sandwich.

"We should be writing this down," Tracy said. "We need to get more people involved. Isabel, you have to think of an event. It could just be a dance or a carnival or something but it would be better if it were something related to your sister. Or something Guatemalan that happens at this time of year."

"How about a fiesta, a Guatemalan festival!" said Isabel. "We could have a fiesta with Guatemalan food and music."

CHAPTER 6

The Festival

The buzzer rang in Isabel's apartment. "Our first houseguest!" Isabel squealed and hugged her mother. She raced downstairs and opened the door for Fernando. "Hi," he said. "I have the lawyer's phone number for you. Her name is June Delgado." He handed Isabel a piece of paper with the immigration lawyer's name and phone number.

"Thanks so much," she said.

"Are the others here?"

"Not yet. Come on upstairs."

A few minutes later Isabel's other new friends arrived, Tracy, Marcus, Ryan, Monique, and Jordan. They all ran upstairs. After saying hello to Isabel's mom they settled down for a meeting. Fernando had named the group the Friends of Guatemala Town Council. The group had already agreed to organize a Guatemalan-style fiesta. The party would be held in November.

The friends had decided that the fiesta would have two goals. The first was to introduce Guatemalan culture to their friends and neighbors. The second was to raise enough money to bring Gloria to Georgia. After two hours of noisy chatter and laughter, the Friends of Guatemala Town Council had put the finishing touches to their fiesta plan.

Isabel felt a new sense of belonging as she waved goodbye to her friends.

In the end, the party was a huge success. Many people had worn traditional Guatemalan clothes. Isabel's mother had prepared mountains of Guatemalan food. Tracy had surprised Isabel and Fernando by finding tapes of Guatemalan music at her mother's library. It seemed that everyone who had been invited came. The guests were charged a small entrance fee, but most gave extra money when they learned what the fiesta was for.

After the fiesta, the exhausted friends stayed behind to help clean up. Suddenly, they heard a loud cheer. Isabel's father rushed in shouting in Spanish. Isabel, her mother, and Fernando all began to dance around the room.

"What's going on?" asked Tracy.

"It's the money!" shouted Isabel. "We have enough money for Gloria's airfare!"

Two weeks later, Isabel stared at the clouded glass door at the airport. She tried to picture her sister on the other side. What did the world look like from an airplane? Isabel wondered. She and her mother had never left the ground. It had taken them more than a week to get from Guatemala to Georgia. Gloria, on the other hand, had been standing in Guatemala just that morning.

What would she think of the United States? Isabel looked out of the airport window. In Guatemala, mountains covered with tropical plants had surrounded her village. Here in Atlanta, there were buildings and roads everywhere. Isabel remembered how the nights in Guatemala were dark and the stars were bright in the sky. Nights in Atlanta were never completely dark. The lights from buildings and cars and shop signs were always shining, pushing back the darkness. Everything was different here in the United States.

Isabel looked at the clothes people were wearing in the airport. They were different from the colorful fabrics used in Guatemalan clothes. The food was different in the United States. The school was different. Isabel knew she could make a list a mile long if she wanted to. Gloria would be as shocked and surprised as she was. She would be overwhelmed. But Isabel had come to love her new home. With any luck her sister would too.

"Are you excited?" asked Fernando.

Isabel smiled. "Are you kidding?"

Fernando laughed. "I'm excited too—and I've never even met her."

"Hey, guys!" Marcus shouted, running down a long corridor with Ryan, Jordan, and Mr. Mann behind. "We got stuck in traffic!"

"Perfect," said Tracy. "Mr. Mann can hold the sign. He's the tallest person here. He can take one end. And . . . Señor Peralta," she said, switching to Spanish. "*¿Hetrero, por favor?*"

"Of course, of course," said Isabel's father taking up one end of the sign. It said "Welcome, Gloria!" in English and Spanish. The Friends of Guatemala Town Council had created it two weeks ago after the success of their fiesta. They had made enough money to send Gloria her airfare. And even better, the immigration lawyer had arranged for Gloria to come right away.

The doors opened. Passengers from the airplane streamed through with bags and luggage. Isabel searched the faces. Her group went quiet as they waited expectantly for Gloria to arrive.

"Gloria!" Isabel's mother shouted.

"Where? Where is she?" shouted Isabel. Out of the crowd of unfamiliar faces Isabel finally saw her sister. Her eyes were wide, confused, afraid.

"Gloria!" Isabel shouted. "Over here!" Gloria turned her head and as she saw her family, she smiled, relieved. She rushed toward them.

"*¡Bienvenidos!* Welcome, Gloria!" Everyone in their group spoke at once as Gloria embraced her mother, her father, and Isabel.

"Isa," Gloria whispered, "who are all these people?"

"They're our new friends," Isabel said. "And they can't wait to meet you."

GUATEMALA IN THE 1980s

Although Isabel and her family are fictional characters, this story is based on actual events. In the 1980s, many Maya families were forced to leave their homes to escape the violence of a civil war. Soldiers burned many villages and killed many people. Fearing for their lives, thousands of Maya fled to Mexico. From there some families moved to the United States.

The Maya The Maya are a group of Native Americans. They have lived in Guatemala for thousands of years. In the tropical rain forest of Guatemala are the ruins of Tikal, a Maya city dating back to 800 B.C. The ancient Maya built a number of cities like Tikal throughout Central America. These had great stone palaces and temples, large plazas, monuments, ball courts, and even saunas. Modern-day Maya have kept many of the traditions of their ancestors, as well as their languages.

Todos Santos Todos Santos is a real village in northwestern Guatemala. The village extends from the top of a mountain plateau down into a river valley. To reach it, visitors must climb a steep, rocky path. Many of the 30,000 people who live in Todos Santos are farmers. They grow corn, beans, squash, and potatoes. The village is famous for its celebration of All Saints Day on November 1. The villagers celebrate with horse races, bands, and dancing.

Guatemalan Weavers

Maya women spin cotton into thread. Then they dye it brilliant colors and weave it to make traditional clothes for their families. They weave symbols and designs into the clothing that tell a story about the person wearing them. For example, the designs might tell that a person is married or how old they are.

Guatemalan Festivals
Guatemalans celebrate many religious festivals. Different villages celebrate in different ways. On All Saints Day in the Guatemalan village of Sacatepéquez, the people fly enormous, colorful kites. On Santos Tomas Day in the town of Chichicastenango, a tall pole is placed in the plaza as part of the celebrations. Young men climb the pole and swing around it on long ropes, often by their feet.

WRITE A PERSONAL LETTER

Imagine you are Isabel. Think about your old life in Guatemala and your new life in Atlanta. What would you tell people about the changes? What has been hardest? What is best?

- Draw a chart like the one below.

- In the first column, list something about Isabel's old life in Todos Santos.

- In the second column list how this is different in Atlanta.

- Use your completed chart to write a letter to a friend. Contrast your life in Guatemala and your life in Atlanta.

In Todos Santos	How this is different in Atlanta
1. Grew our own food	1. Buy food from the store
2. Didn't feel safe, afraid of soldiers	2. Not afraid of the police

READ MORE ABOUT THE SOUTHEAST

Find and read more books about the history of the Southeast. As you read, think about these questions. They will help you understand more about this topic.

- Why do people want to leave the country they live in?

- What problems do immigrants face when they move to the United States?

- Which immigrant groups have moved to the Southeast?

- How has the Southeast changed over time?

SUGGESTED READING
Reading Expeditions
Travels Across America's Past
The Southeast: Its History and People